THE

PURPOSE

OF

EXISTENCE

THE PURPOSE OF EXISTENCE

How I Discovered My Purpose

CLAVER LUKOKI

Copyright © 2019. All rights reserved.

No part of this publication may be reproduced, stored in a retrieval system or transmitted in any way by any means, electronic, mechanical, photocopy, recording or otherwise, without the prior permission of the author except as provided by USA copyright law.

Published by Greater Works Publishing

www.greaterworkspublishing.com

Greater Works Publishing is committed to excellence in the publishing industry.

Book design Copyright © 2019 by Greater Works Publishing. All rights reserved.

Published in the United States of America

Paperback: 978-1-68411-690-4

Hardcover: 978-0-359-33188-8

IN MEMORY OF MY GRANDMA

ANGELIQUE MAWONZO

1918-2018

ACKNOWLEDGEMENTS

First and foremost, I would like to thank my Lord Jesus Christ. In the process of putting this book together, I realised how privileged I am and how I have been favoured enough to write this book. Through the Holy Spirit, I have been enabled to have deeper insights and revelations of the word and a knowing of my purpose. None of this would have been accomplished without my Father God. Therefore, I thank you Lord God for giving me the power to believe in my passion and pursue my purpose and dreams. Without the Grace and the Mercy of the Lord, I would not have been able to finalise this book.

To my Father and Mother, Kiyedi Lukombo and Kimbinga Mpembele Lukombo: I am truly blessed to call you my parents. I have come to the realisation that words are not enough to express my gratitude for all the wisdom, love and support you have given me. You are and have always been my number one fans and for that, I am eternally grateful. I pray that I will be a good parent to my children as you were and have always been to me.

To my brothers and sisters, I just want to say that I deeply love you all from the depths of my heart. You all have always made me feel appreciated and loved at all times. I am amazed by your support always and I pray that this book will also help you to discover your ultimate purpose in Christ and live it out for the glory of God in Jesus Christ our Lord.

To my little brother Bradley and Nephew Omari: my only prayer for you both is that as you two grow older, that you will come into the knowledge of Christ Jesus and pursue him alone for the rest of your life. That you two will know and fulfil your purpose to the LORD your God. Obey his directions, laws, commands, rules, and written instructions as they are recorded in His word. Then you'll succeed in everything you do wherever you go. I love you both always.

My sincere thanks to my pastors, Bishop Abel Success Kungu, Pastor Freddy, Lillian Maleka and Pastor Zorka Crichlow: I just want to say I am forever grateful and thankful for your continuous patience, love and prayers.

You all have given your lives to serve and support individuals like myself, thank you for believing in me and for the gift that has been bestowed upon you by the Lord to glorify Him.

I thank my fellow youths at TODFAN, thank you for all your support and encouragement. You are the best and you have all motivated me to grow in my walk with the Lord. I pray that this book will also empower you to walk in your purpose.

To my fiancé, Petrena Notice: You are one of the main reasons why I wrote this book. I am so thankful that I have you in my life, pushing me during my weakest moments. I thank you for standing beside me throughout the process of writing this book, I enjoyed writing it. You have been my inspiration and motivation for continuing to improve my knowledge and move forward with my purpose. You are more than an angel and I am overly blessed by God to have you by my side. All the good that comes from this book, I look forward to sharing with you. Thanks for believing in me, particularly believing that I could complete this book. My love for you will continue to grow.

Finally, a big thank you to all my other family and friends. Although, I did not precisely mention your names, all your support and encouragement has been invaluable.

FOREWORD

by Chis'mere Mallard

One of life's biggest questions is, "Why am I here?" We all face this quandary at some time in our lives and some of us never seem to find the answer. We often find something to occupy our time, but that's not the same as finding our true purpose in life. That's a different adventure to embark on.

For some, the circumstances of life can make this journey of self-discovery harder than it is for most of us. Situations and events try to steer us in the wrong direction, telling us that we are someone we are not. Other people around us can do the same thing too, especially those who are closest to us.

However, if we are ever going to be successful and achieve all that we can do, we must realise who we are and what we were created to be. We need to find our purpose - not a general purpose or one that was enforced on us by others or by circumstances, but the one that is known by God Almighty.

God Himself has established the purpose for your life; no one else. Only He knows the full potential that He has placed in each one of us. He wrote the story before it even began, waiting for us to fulfill it. When we go to Him to seek that purpose, we find true answers - answers that give us our reason to live.

Claver Lukoki has made that journey - a journey of discovery to find his true purpose. His story brings to light the many things that can go wrong on that path, as well as things that may go right. As we identify with his life, it can help us find the things in our own lives that have led us on detours, pushing us off the path we were intended to tread. Along the way, we can also find how to navigate back onto the right path.

Join Claver on this journey, a path of purpose and destiny, as you seek to become familiar with your own path of purpose.

Your path is waiting, are you ready to walk it?

Are you ready to find the true potential of what you were created to be?

FOREWORD

By Vinette Hoffman-Jackson

Jeremiah 29:11

"For I know the plans that I have for you,' declares the Lord, 'plans for welfare and not for calamity to give you a future and a hope". [NASB]

It was Harold S. Kushner who wrote the bestselling book 'When Bad Things Happen to Good People' which addresses a poignant question that everyone at some point in their lives asks themselves, but especially people of a particular faith or religion 'Why do bad things happen to good people?'

The fundamental belief held by many is the religious or spiritual persuasion that good things are rewards for good people and bad things happen as punishment to bad people. It is one of the premises of most religions. It is therefore inevitable that one will begin to question their faith or shadows of doubts may creep in, when faced with seemingly insurmountable obstacles and when their cries to God seem futile and appear not go beyond the immediate surrounding atmosphere. It is in these dark moments that a man is truly tested to prove himself worthy of his existence. Through this roller coaster of suffering and triumph it serves to give some credence to the existence of a greater force in the Universe.

Claver in his debut book tackles this gargantuan task that has permeated the history of mankind from when the records of time began; in his search for the meaning of his existence. He takes you on a deeply personal journey through the darkest periods of his life when it seemed like the entire world was conspiring against his very existence and his mental sanity. Faced with challenges that seem to originate beyond the scope of our physical world, his thoughts shift to his only perceived viable option of total self-destruction. He speaks frankly about his consideration of suicide as he loses all hope.

The book embraces a language and style that aids in the cognitive processing of the emotions felt by the author and you are able to see the world through the eyes of a young Christian man. He shares with us the restoration and re-ignition of his faith in God and his journey to overcome the many battles he faced.

Claver's book is relatable to almost anyone, whether or not they are religiously inclined, his stories are captivating and represent real life experiences that are easily identifiable by many today. He subconsciously teases the social conscience of our generation with a subtle reminder of the dangers of assuming everything is okay behind a person's smile.

His book is also void of the usual happy endings that are synonymous with fairy tales. Claver realistically chooses to divulge to us that he still has unfinished battles but now feels better equipped to deal with them. He openly embraces and acknowledges the presence of the Lord in his life and his promise to be with him always.

An excellent read for all.

Isaiah 43:2

*"When you pass through the waters, I will be with you;
And through the rivers, they will not overflow you.
When you walk through the fire, you will not be scorched,
Nor will the flame burn you". [NASB]*

THE PURPOSE OF EXISTENCE showcases the comforting reassurance and the inner peace of a man who has indeed found the true purpose of his existence.

Vinette Hoffman-Jackson is an award-winning international speaker and has represented the U.K. & Ireland as a speaker. She is the author of the bestselling books 'Did the Right Sperm Win? Books 1 & 2 and Behind my Smile. She is currently completing her studies to become a qualified social psychologist. She is a Speaker /Author /Trainer.

Table of Contents

Acknowledgements vi

Foreword by Chis'mere Mallard xi

Foreword by Vinette Hoffman-Jackson xiii

Preface xix

Introduction xxiii

Chapter 1 // **Absent** 1

Chapter 2 // **Changing Perceptions** 11

Chapter 3 // **Broken Friendships** 17

Chapter 4 // **Criticism** 21

Chapter 5 // **Walk The Walk** 25

Chapter 6 // **The Challenges Within The Purpose** 31

Chapter 7 // **To Love And Be Loved** 35

Chapter 8 // **The New Me** 41

Chapter 9 // **Moving On** 47

Chapter 10 // **A Word Of Advice** 53

Chapter 11 // **Final Thoughts** 57

About The Author 61

Preface

There is absolutely nothing in this world more frustrating than not knowing or understanding your identity - who you truly are and the purpose of your life. I truly believe that whether we like it or not, this question of purpose tends to have power over everything that surrounds our daily lives as it constructs us to act and behave accordingly. When we have no clear idea of who we are, we base who we should be on the image that society presents to us.

Consequently, we live our lives behind the identity of other people - imitating their identity, rather than spending the time to discover who we really are. That is why it is important to live a purpose-driven life. Many of us battle with self-image, hence why we adore celebrities and compare ourselves to them. Surprisingly, those we look to for guidance also struggle to find their purpose here on Earth. So, we end up with misconceptions of who we truly are.

Like many of us, in my younger years, I struggled to understand the purpose of my existence and my identity. I felt the urge to perceive why God created me, and why I could not fit in with others. Even after my water baptism and commitment to the Lord in Christianity, I still desired for my questions to be answered. The void I felt before was still there even after becoming a Christian, so I began to pray and ask the Lord to reveal Himself and the meaning behind my existence. I began to acknowledge that there is more to life than waking up and going to work. I started asking the Lord these five questions through my journey of discovery: who am I? I believe there are hundreds of millions of people around the world in every language, race, and culture asking these questions because they want to know who they are. Where am I from? Every human being naturally wants to discover where they came from. Why am I here? All of us want to understand our purposes on this planet earth; are we just here to live and die and that's it. What can I do? What is my true ability? They say the average human only uses 10% of their brain. No one seems to know their true ability. Where am I going? It seems as if there is a mystery to this question that every human being still does not comprehend.

These questions and many more inspired me to write this book. In my own personal life, there were so many occasions where I completely felt like giving up, saying to myself that 'this life is not for me'. I was really in a dark place where I felt like the enemy was really coming up after me to take everything I had and to turn everything and everybody against me. You see, when the calling of God is upon your life, you automatically become the target of the enemy and his workers. Still, the Lord kept me all the way through these dark seasons of my life until today and made me understand and see the purpose of my existence. There are still a couple of things that I am fighting through, but this time I'm not fighting alone, for the Lord is with me to give me victory in every area of my life.

In my book, I have identified my hurt, pain, struggle and everything else that some of you may know nothing about. This shows that healing is real and is for you to receive today and right now.

INTRODUCTION

God is our Master and Creator of all things; He is a perfect organiser and He knows how to call a man to Himself. Jesus Christ came to the Earth and gave His life for the salvation of mankind. This happened over two thousand years ago, yet not everyone on Earth has acknowledged this. Thank God for His different strategies of calling us to Himself - and most times, He does this through our personal experiences.

The Bible is replete with testimonies of people who suffered different adversities that led to their encounters with God, which eventually set them on their paths to the discovery and fulfilling of their purpose. For Moses, who was trained in the best army of his day, who rose through the ranks to become an army general, God had to set a bush on fire to get his attention! That single incident placed him on his path to discovering and achieving his purpose on Earth.

The Purpose Of Existence

Joseph, one of the sons of Jacob, had a dream of becoming a leader of some sort; he didn't really know his purpose at the time of the dream, but as events unfolded in his life, his brothers sold him into slavery and he found himself in Egypt. When he was sold into slavery, it was adversity that led him to be the chief servant in the house of Potiphar. He enjoyed his life for a little while, but adversity struck again and sent him to prison, where he eventually met the man who told the Pharaoh about him, allowing him to finally arrive at his destination and become the first deliverer of Israel.

Genesis 45:6-8

"For the famine has been in the land these two years, and there are still five years in which there will be neither plowing nor harvesting. ⁷ God sent me before you to preserve for you a remnant in the earth, and to keep you alive by a great deliverance. ⁸ Now, therefore, it was not you who sent me here, but God; and He has made me a father to Pharaoh and lord of all his household and ruler over all the land of Egypt". [NASB]

David was raised by God to be the shepherd king of Israel, yet nobody knew him or recognised him as king until there was the encounter with Goliath. This brought him to the limelight and set him on the path to discovering and fulfilling his purpose. Today we are glad that David fulfilled his purpose and became the ancestor of our Lord.

Everything there is on Earth today was created, fabricated or manufactured for a purpose and the only way to achieve the highest potential on Earth is through the fulfilment of purpose. Gold is refined through intense heat and fire; this is exactly what happens to so many of us on Earth - we discover our purpose and the best of us begins to manifest in adversity.

This book is a life testimony of how I discovered my purpose in God through adverse life experiences in my youth and I am grateful to God that I had to go through everything I will recount in this book. Those experiences brought me to Christ, helped me discover my purpose in life and formed the man whose drive now is to help others discover their purpose in God.

It may be that you are in a place today where you are wondering about your reason for being? I know you have gone through a lot in your life and probably have a lot of questions that need answers. I am glad to declare to you that the God of heaven created you for a purpose; you are not a speck in the dust; you are not just a product of your parents; there is a unique purpose for your existence. God has a plan for you and He has sent me to help you unravel the mysteries of your life through this book.

It is my prayer that as you travel with me through the pages of this book, you will realise that God has been working out His good pleasures in you through the adversities you may have been faced with. I pray that you will suddenly come into the realisation and fulfilment of your God-given purpose on Earth. In Jesus' name, amen!

Chapter 1

Absent

First, let me take you back, we lived in the capital city of Congo, Kinshasa, in a town called N'djili. I was born at a hospital nearby. Big and healthy, I was well received by my family. We lived in a compound with my extended family. I would describe our status as middle class, in that all our material needs were met; my father was known to be a hardworking man and so he played this part very well.

When I was a child, there were many things I didn't understand – things about people; about families; and about the way things should be done. I didn't understand the dynamics of my household at all - I just grew up knowing my family as the sum of its members: two parents and siblings. The older I grew, the more I started to recognise certain things, and the more I became aware of the relationship between my mother and father.

I will describe my father first: he seemed to be a nice person, but he and I did not relate very well. I could never fully understand who he was, because whenever he was home, he was engaged with other things. His only interaction with us was to give an instruction or to tell us what we needed to learn. I don't remember really sitting down with my father and just laughing or playing games together; I don't remember spending nice quality time with my father the way a child is supposed to.

But behind the seemingly sensible and pleasant façade, my father's relationship with my mother was quite different. For her, his homecoming would be tarred by physical abuse. I remember him pushing her whilst being pregnant with my little brother and throwing things at her in front of other people. I will never forget the times he would insult her in front of us.

When this would happen, there would be an intense rage growing in my heart, but I would not be able to do anything to stop him. All I could do was observe; I had to hide my feelings and just watch the abuse while the anger welled up inside me. I recall feeling like I didn't want to do anything with him - the recurring image I would have was of just burying him. Bitterness was being moulded in my heart.

I remember my mother working so hard at home for us, doing chore after chore and working to make sure that we were all doing well. She would wake up and make sure we were fed, clean the house and take us to school. She was a well-groomed woman who did her best to 'make a house a home'. Nevertheless, it seemed as though there were two pictures in our household, the way we perceived things to be and the actual reality of their marriage.

I believe my mother knew what kind of man she had married and was trying to shield and protect us to keep us from being hurt by him or his absence. She did this by taking a deep interest in our lives. She would always talk to us and show her concern about the things we were going through. Her affection for us deepened through this process, and I know she always strove to emphasise her love for us. Although I didn't see it at the time, looking back, I am able to recognise my father's absence, and I realise now that I felt the same as those children who were raised by a single mother, in the same way that they never had a father around. I felt like my father was in the house, but still not really there; we were emotionally detached and there was no intimacy or affection between us. We just coexisted; we were not really a family in the way a family is meant to be.

Now I see that he was not fathered properly too. The way he fathered us is the same as he experienced growing up; it was how he was raised and all he knew. I can see the pattern as it carried from one generation to another. Our parents just parent us the best way they know how, and many times they come with their own wounds and backgrounds that are not good. They can't help but to reflect their own childhood experiences, and that is what I saw my father doing. But I really sought after that love and affection; I really sought after that relationship; I really wanted us to be close.

I was so curious about my father. I wanted to know what he thought about different things; I wanted his opinion on the things that were going on in my life - I wish that I had gotten advice from him back then and that we could've sometimes sat down and had a laugh together. But it was very difficult to do that. There was no time - everything was just straightforward, and routine-based:

the wife stays at home and does the housework while the husband goes out to earn the money. That's just how we grew up. Nevertheless, the things I went through with my parents are those same very things that have helped me in my journey with God. Through these things, I have been able to find myself; and I have found my identity in God. My father did not show me my identity or affirm who I was because we just did not have that kind of relationship or bond. As a result, I feared men and hated them. I did not want their influence or their advice. I started believing that they must be weak and cowardly. At the same time, another mindset began to form inside of me. There was a perception that maybe women were not as valuable and that they could be treated recklessly. I grew up with a posture to abuse women, because that's all I had known and seen at home.

As for my mother, I never really knew much about her upbringing - I just came to know her as the mother that she was to us. I know that she was loving, that she looked after us, and that she had deep affections for us. At the time, I could see such pain in her face; I could see that sometimes she was quite absent from us; I could see that she was a woman who wanted nothing but love. She desired for more, but there were times I could see the depression clouding her face and her demeanour. I don't know how she managed, but she just got on with life regardless - sucked it all in and took on every challenge that came towards her.

She sacrificed and sacrificed, loved and loved on us. Nevertheless, I could tell that she, too, needed the same love and attention that she was giving. My parents were absent in different ways - it was not a matter of who did more or who did less. I am saying all this so that you can identify with me and hopefully see your own journey in mine.

I believe that my mother was tired of the lifestyle she had, always seeking a better future for herself. I could tell that she would contemplate the life she had at the time, perhaps even compare her marital life to other couples' and households. I assume she felt helpless and that's why she didn't take any action; the thought that things may never change must have haunted her.

The relationship we built together was good, but you could see that it was not ideal, because a child should not just be attached to one parent. They must have good relationships with both. I never had that balance, and so I would always run to my mum rather than my dad whenever I found myself in any trouble.

In certain situations, when a child is scared, it is more common for them to look to their dad rather than mum to keep them safe. Traditionally, the mother is sought for comfort and nurture, while the father is and should be the protector of a family. Those roles had become blurred for me and as a boy, I found myself constantly seeking all of this support from mum. Whether it was about bullying, fallouts, or being scorned and mistreated by friends, through all that, I kept on confiding and seeking refuge in her. Of course, she was supportive, but this interaction had resulted in an abnormal mother-son relationship. I had become my mother's substitute mate; we found each other as a source of comfort, and as a child, I had taken my father's place at my mother's side. I can now see that they did not have that closeness in their marriage. They were together but were only together because it served a particular purpose. Mum just needed someone to listen. She was a woman who craved that quality time - and we both found that in each other.

In hindsight, it is obvious that one parent was more involved in our upbringing than the other. I felt that my mum made more of the effort, but I can see now that she did a lot of things out of fear. She wanted us protected and cared so much for us, but it was also such a heavy burden to look after us emotionally without my dad. I don't blame him for his absence; I just think that he had a traditional way of raising children. They both influenced my life and upbringing no matter how I felt or how I saw things. They both played their role in different ways; both shaped my life, and both shaped my identity in an unknown way. As I grew up and started to become independent, I realised that the identity they gave me was not enough.

Looking back, a lot of things were distorted in my life because of my experiences as a child. I began to prefer female friends rather than males. I felt that I could confide in them, perhaps trust them more than males. On the other hand, I found myself in a whirlwind of perversion. The void that was created in my heart drew me to sexual addictions, hatred and bitterness. I started treating women like sex toys; I treated them like nothing. I just thought 'I can have sex anyhow without any consequences', but these actions were wrecking my life and widening that void that only Jesus could fill. I became addicted to sex, pornography and women. I had no purpose; I allowed life to define me. But God was calling me for something greater.

I needed to search deeper and find my true identity, otherwise everything else was speaking into and shaping my identity - a false identity. I just wanted to know who I was called to be and what I was meant to do on this earth; I needed and wanted something more because my thinking, my culture - everything was shaped by my upbringing. I needed God to come in and reshape my mindset; I needed to base my identity in Him.

"You can decorate absence however you want- but you will still feel what's missing."
-Siobhan Vivian

Chapter 2
Changing Perceptions

From what I've already mentioned, it's obvious that I had very different relationships with each of my parents. I experienced their absence, both emotionally and, sometimes, physically. I started seeing that this also affected how I viewed other people. As I grew up and went to school, college, and then university, I realised that my perceptions of others were cynical.

I discovered that I harboured a lot of mistrust. It was hard for people to get into my space and inner circle; I wanted them to prove themselves to me before I would allow them to get close. I had this issue throughout childhood, and into adulthood I could see that it was very difficult for me to let go of this mind-set. I could see that it was very difficult for me to open my heart to people or tell them how I felt. I could see that this was affecting me because at the end of it, I was experiencing complete loneliness. All I longed for were deep conversations with people; I longed to have an intimate relationship with someone - and sometimes that longing would get me into trouble.

One time, I met a lady in church and we became close. I would see her around and greet her, and as time went on we started to build a relationship. We would call and message each other and even meet up for regular chats. I would tell her all my struggles. It felt so easy to talk to her: she just took the time to listen to me without judging me. I found so much comfort in that. I opened up to her because this was familiar behaviour to me - perhaps you could say that I was looking for another "mother figure" to connect with.

As much as this connection was completely innocent, however, it didn't take long before I was accused of having an affair with her. Her husband approached me and warned me to stay away. It was a difficult time in my life. I just needed somewhere to offload my problems - something I found difficult to do with men. Actually, I generally found this difficult to do regardless, and that woman had been an exception. She had let me in to her space as well, so it was easier for me to feel comfortable with her. I've always been cautious not to open up until the other person has opened up to me, as I have carried so many fears and anxieties, worries about people betraying my confidence. I would always imagine the worst-case scenario.

I mainly resisted men. I could not talk with a man face-to-face; I could not sit with a man for too long. It just felt uncomfortable. I would not take any advice from a man – I had built a complete wall between myself and other men. I could not even befriend them for a while. When my elders told me things or gave me advice, internally I would just reject or discard whatever they had to say. I would assume a defensive posture that just pushed them away, creating a gap between us. So, I could see that my perception of people was really disoriented. I needed some sort of healing; I needed a new perception and I needed to know who I was. I also knew that this issue was destroying my relationship with Father God, because I had begun to adopt the same posture towards Him.

At that time in my life, I found it hard to engage with Him. I struggled to talk to God and lean on Him. He was right in front of me, and yet I continued to find other ways to get help. Often, I would search for other ways and methods besides His help without even realising. My father issues and male walls prevented me from engaging with Father God and trusting Him. It was really a depressive time of my life and I knew that I had a great need to really discover myself.

In one of my sessions with my mentor, he asked me this question, "Why do you find it so hard to sit down with your pastor to talk about everything that you are feeling?" I started thinking, and so I asked God the same question. Right there and then, the Holy Spirit revealed to me that the absence of such a connection with my biological father had greatly affected me, and as a result, I had resorted to keeping everything to myself.

Psychologically, this pattern has been observed in children: if your relationships at home are broken, it becomes very difficult to build them elsewhere. A similar pattern is also observed theologically: a broken relationship between dad and child affects the child's relationship with Father God in the same way.

At that time, the Lord reminded me that it took me a very long time to open up to Him and tell Him, "Father, this is how I am feeling..." I remember on one occasion, God started speaking to me about sonship, about the reason why He created fathers on this planet. He said it was for them to reflect His fatherhood and to show us how the love of an earthly father can help us experience His own.

He told me that I don't need to fix myself; I don't need to act in a certain way to have a conversation with Him. That was what helped me to understand that just like I don't need to be afraid to talk to my dad, I don't need to be afraid to talk to my Heavenly Father as a son - that's what made it so easy for me to understand the importance of sonship when it comes to having a conversation with your father; that is what really helped my relationships with both God and my earthly father to progress.

We need to understand that the word 'sonship' has a greater meaning than we may think. Sonship is about inheritance, identity and position. When God calls you into sonship, He is saying, "Lay everything down." It is a higher calling than just becoming His son through salvation. It's about Him becoming the Lord over your life.

Luke 14:26 says:

"If anyone comes to Me and does not hate his own father and mother and wife and children and brothers and sisters, yes, and even his own life, he cannot be My disciple." [NASB]

Jesus was saying that if you want to tap into the depths of your inheritance you must lay your life down completely: nothing and no one should be more important than Him and when you do that. He will mould you into your true identity and place you in the right position so that you can fulfil your destiny. That's what this calling is all about, and so I realised God was taking me on to a peculiar path.

"If you cannot change your condition, change your perception."

- Debasish Mridha

CHAPTER 3
Broken friendships

Going back to my childhood, specifically when I was ten years old, a certain event greatly amplified the fears I had about people. I had a friend I deeply loved and honoured. I thought, 'Wow! I finally have a friend that I can trust, and we can do everything together!' He came to my house, I went to his, our mums knew each other - it was the perfect match! I could finally love and trust someone! However, my family were not too impressed with him. They didn't really like him, and I could not understand why. I did not know that this friend of mine had an agenda. He had a secret.

One day, we visited a church where there was a woman who had been given a prophetic word over my life. God had shown her that something was wrong - she could tell that someone was trying to kill me. So, she approached me and asked me about my friend. She even described every detail about him. She revealed that my friend was planning to ritually sacrifice me to gain supernatural power. When I heard what she said, my heart sank. I could not believe the betrayal.

It seemed as though things were getting even worse when it came to my relationships. My perceptions of people were not getting better either. All the trust I had built up in my new friend disappeared. I felt like I could not love anymore. I was speechless. Why did this person try to do this to me? What about me was worth taking my life? It broke my heart. I distanced myself from people even further. My mother on the other hand was angry; she couldn't believe what was happening. So, we rushed over to his house. His mother confronted him, and he admitted to the whole thing. He said that he was going to sacrifice me for power. Worse still, I discovered that my cousin was involved in this devious plot against me. From that time, I felt very alone.

That was the end of our relationship. My mum did not want him around me - and I couldn't face him either. My anger would often erupt on the inside. I may not have said much about it all, but within I harboured bitterness and hatred. I needed to distance myself from the whole thing. Throughout all those experiences, I kept asking myself, "Who am I?"; "What am I meant to do here on earth?"; "Who do I love?"; "Who will love me?"

I vowed to myself never to trust people again – not even friends. I experienced so much loneliness in my life. Even while I was growing up, I only had friends because I had to - because I felt that I needed to, not because I wanted them or thought it would be enjoyable. So, I squeezed my way into other groups of friends as time went on.

"The worst pain in the world goes beyond the physical. Even further beyond any other emotional pain one can feel, it is the betrayal of a friend."

CHAPTER 4
Criticism

None of us like criticism, though I'm sure all of us have been through our fair share of it, whether it's from your family, friends or colleagues. Everybody goes through those experiences of being judged and criticised. I must say that criticism, just like rejection, is probably one of the hardest things a human being can deal with. The problem is that when you don't know or believe in yourself, it can really affect you and destroy you; it can end up defining you and turning you into a bitter person - a person who just stays away from people. Through my experiences with people, parents and friends, I started to see a certain pattern emerging in my life. I could see that all my relationships were being cut short in same way. They would fail to produce the fruit they were meant to produce: a disturbance, an offence or some breakdown would always occur.

The enemy was attacking my relationships. He knew that if they were attacked, there was no way I was going to make it with God. I was called to be a relational person. So, he came after my relationships - all of them! This was his biggest assignment over my life.

God also made me to be a healer. That means to heal relationships, hearts, and physical bodies. I am called to advise people and encourage people; to evangelise people into the Kingdom. All of those things require relationships; they require a person who can relate to people very well. But the enemy had planned to place sticks and stones on my path, to divert me and make me into someone who hates and rejects people.

He had orchestrated my life so that I could be hurt by people, full of hate and bitterness so that those things would hinder my destiny. There was no way I would be able to evangelise or encourage other people; it would not happen.

So here I was again, at 25 years old, and I had started experiencing ridicule from my friends. At first, I thought they were good, that they were cool. They seemed to have nice girls and nice clothes. Once I joined their group, though, I found that they were actually mean: they said bad things about me; they mocked and shamed me. Yet, because I wanted to be in their group so much, I just stayed there and accepted their ridicule. I even imitated them and tried to blend in just to please them. All of this was because I had that need to be wanted and accepted. This behaviour was rooted in my childhood: if you do not feel accepted or needed when you are young, you will always seek that feeling when you become older. I found that I was constantly in need of that - I *needed* companionship; I *needed* quality time; yet I could not let go of the judgments I held against people.

So, I stayed in those circles despite the disgrace I faced every day. It did not stop; it kept going and it was as if I could never learn my lesson. It was hard for me to handle their constant criticism. At times I would sit by myself and just cry. I thought to myself, "Why is my life like this?"; "Why do people hate me?"; "Why don't they love me for who I am?" I just wanted to be someone else - not Mario; not me - someone else that was just liked. However, it was in that darkness that I found out my flaws; I discovered the things that were affecting me, and I knew that none of these things could make me into what I wanted to be. I realised that only God could take me out of that situation, and that only He could affirm me. So, through my life experiences I was brought to a place where I kept questioning and asking God, "Who am I?"; "What am I meant to do?" Without purpose, there is no life; without purpose, there is no hope and no joy - because a man is fulfilled in his purpose. I just wanted to know what God called me to do so that I could get to that place – and stay there. Then things in my life would be better. I would not need to rely on people, relationships or any of the other things I was wrongly depending on.

The final proof of greatness lies in being able to endure criticism without resentment.

— Elbert Hubbard

CHAPTER 5

Walk the walk

As you can see, my path has been a difficult one. I have had to learn many hard lessons along the way and pass through many fires. All the while, all I really wanted was to discover who I am, and in doing so, I eventually realised I needed to own my life - I had to choose what I wanted. I had come to see that I was living through other people and looking to them to give me what I needed. It was during this time that I had come to know the Lord Jesus Christ. One night, on my way to the club, I began to hear this voice speaking to me. He was asking me questions such as, *"What are you doing in this place?"* and *"Why are you even here? What will you get from this place?"* I kept dismissing the thoughts but then afterwards, when walking home, to my surprise the questions kept coming: *"What are doing with your life?"* I found this strange and rather startling, but I knew it was God calling me. So, when I got home, I begun to pray, and

I made this prayer to the Lord saying "I don't know what I'm doing with my life but I just pray don't kill me, please" As I was praying, I started to sweat profusely, and I had an experience as though something was coming out of body. This lasted until five am, and by then I was exhausted - I thought, "Let me just rest for a bit," but as soon as I closed my eyes, I had a terrifying open vision that I was dragging myself into Hell without knowing. After this bizarre encounter, I surrendered my whole life to Jesus that very morning and *everything* changed for me. I became acquainted with a local church, and I embarked on this journey called Christianity.

I started believing in God's word and Who He said He was. I also had powerful encounters with Him, yet I still sensed that I had not really grasped what I needed to about Him at the time. Even when I went to church, I thought to myself, *"Who is this man?"* All I knew was that He saved me from sin. He saved me from my wrong ways and took me from darkness to light. I started wondering and questioning whether there was more to know: *"There must be more to this walk of Christianity"*; *"There must be more to learn, more to understand and experience"*. I felt like everything in the church was always the same and even though I was from a Christian family, I still lacked knowledge.

Eventually I started to lose my way again, though, finding it harder and harder to connect with God. My passion started to die, and I began to lose sight of the whole concept of Christianity and of who Jesus was. Enthusiastic pursuit faded and turned to bland indifference. I couldn't figure it out - God seemed to keep taking me through all these different journeys; so many unexpected ups and downs, and yet it was on these journeys that I seemed to be rediscovering myself. The only constant was that I had no one to really lean on, except for Him.

I was an adult; I could not run to my mother. All I had now was God, and I began to realise that He wanted me to be in that place of loneliness for a reason. He wanted me to only look to Him, to depend on Him. I had depended on so many other things up until that point, but now He was removing them from me. As this happened, I gradually came to know how wonderful He is. He started unravelling who I was, and I started to understand more about the person I had become and the person He wanted me to be. It felt like a long process - like a path where many things did not make sense, but day after day I could feel Him speaking to my heart. I could feel Him affirming me, showing me my passions and His calling on my life.

We all need to know that finding your purpose is *not* just about finding your career. It is very much about knowing your identity in God - which means knowing that you are a son (or daughter), that you have a kingdom to rule and that you have authority. You are not meant to be controlled by the things and the people around you. Such things are not meant to oppress or distract you - and even if they do, you are able to quickly rise above, because you are a child of God. It is about knowing your spiritual rights, the tools and weapons that He has given you to overcome. It is about understanding Biblical truths, and maturing in those truths. It is about understanding that God created you in His image. We are powerful beings in His name.

Remember that in the beginning, God gave human beings the authority to name animals. Adam could name them. He had that authority to speak over other species. This is what the enemy has stolen from us - he has stolen this knowledge so that he can continue to make us feel like victims instead of victors. He wants to keep you in a place of hopelessness, in a place where you feel that you cannot change the way you are. The enemy wants to be your ruler, but Jesus has come to see that you have a choice. Through Christ, I can take charge over my own life and I do not have to take on my childhood experiences - the betrayals, the bullying - as part of my identity.

The second part of your purpose in Christ is about your written scroll in heaven. The psalmist refers to a book that contains all the days of your life. God knows what you ought to become and that's what we call a scroll:

Psalms 139:16

"Your eyes have seen my unformed substance; And in Your book were all written the days that were ordained for me, when as yet there was not one of them". [NASB]

A scroll holds the missions God has called you to on this Earth. It might include being called to worship, business, education and so forth. These things will not work without sonship. You must understand that you are a child of God and recognise what He has put in your hands. Our scrolls consist of the gifts He has given to us and it is our responsibility to cooperate with Him fully so that we can achieve in the things He has called us to.

God kept talking to my heart about this - about the passions deep inside of me. For those that were hidden, I just felt the Father's encouragement. He made me believe in myself, made me understand His love for me. I feared Him and feared His love due to my brokenness; His love for me was overwhelming. In that lonely place, His love burnt like fire. I could just feel Him loving on me. For the first time, I felt that genuine concern coming from a man, from a father. It really empowered me to go and search for more. My life has been driven by so many of those moments where God has spoken to me personally - where He has ministered to my heart about who I am, leading me forth.

"The habit of talking the talk has distracted many people from walking the walk."

— **Edmond Mbiaka**

CHAPTER 6

The Challenges within the Purpose

I found that my days were getting brighter and things were starting to look up - it was as if I was coming out of that dark place. It was so extreme, and it was so intense that I did not feel like going back there, but I was glad about the things that I had discovered. I felt that I had really come to understand God's mercy, His love and His desire to be with us all the time. He is always on our side; He wants us to defeat the enemy. I felt so much encouragement from that season even though at the time, I was not doing well emotionally, physically and circumstantially. I believe that season was there for a reason - God wanted to show me something. I needed to be in a place of solitude to really hear what He had to say.

I felt excited that I had found something new to Christianity. I felt like, "Yes! I can go and pursue my passions!" I wanted to do music; I wanted to write; I wanted to rap - I wanted to do things for the Kingdom. Those were the things that He had called me to, but it was not that easy to step into them. I faced my fair share of challenges; realising that first I needed so much training in all these areas, I started to question whether I really understood all the concepts that God was talking to me about. How do you learn to be a son (or daughter) of God? Sonship does not just come when you get saved. You must learn to be a son; it's a process. Your sonship will show through your obedience to God. So, I realised there was much more to that revelation than I thought. I had to learn to be a son and work hard on my passions.

I had to fully commit myself to God; I had to give my all to Him. I could not afford to be half-hearted or go back and forth. I had to pursue Him whole-heartedly. I guess my solution to that was to immerse myself into ministry. At that point, I started being active in the church. I thought, "Let me dive into singing"; "Let me dive into some business strategies"; "Let me dive into the work that's being done here at the church and that will keep me committed". So, I did. Nonetheless, it was all a challenge. Ministerial positions require a lot of character adjustments: humility, patience and so on. They are not positions you can simply acquire; you have to be disciplined in the Lord.

So, there I was, working with people in ministry. I had to face my issue of people once again: taking instructions from people, being in a crowd and being led by other authority figures. I recognised that I needed to deal with my pride - I wanted to lead and not follow others. God used this platform to prune me again so that He could use me. It was such a significant process - God had to cut off some of my perspectives. He had to show me what humility looks like and He showed me that I must forgive others. I had to let go of the bitterness and the anger - the things of the past. I had to learn to love others the same way He loved me.

I understood that I could not fulfil my purpose without people; I could not fulfil my purpose without other people's advice or influence, encouragement or their directives. So again, it was like God took me away to talk to me and when I came back, He made me face all my issues and fears. This time, though, I was much more prepared than before. I had learnt a lot. He could now guide me; He could show me how to deal with them.

The Purpose Of Existence

We are called to love, it is the purpose of our existence to do so. So, God taught me that I had to learn both to love and to be loved by others and in that process, I met someone who was willing to walk that journey with me. I met my fiancée. She had so much patience for me then, and having grown since the time we met, I can see how she has contributed to the maturity I'm now walking in.

It's been a rollercoaster journey, but I feel that God has thoroughly dealt with me! Many great things have come out of that place. So, I would say God humbled me until I learnt to work with people; until I learnt to let go of hurts and pains. Did you know that when we hold onto unforgiveness, it's all really just pride? God cannot come in and do anything with us if we are holding onto those things. God worked in me to destroy that pride and I was able to break through.

"Life is full of challenges, but these challenges are only given to you because God knows your faith is strong enough to get you through them."

CHAPTER 7

To Love and be Loved

Meeting my fiancée took me to another level in terms of knowing myself. I think when I was getting to know her, I had so much confidence. I thought I knew what women were like, because of my relationship with my mum. So, I assumed it would be the same with her. How naïve was I? She was not like the other women I had been with. I had to adjust to her way of doing things, and there are some things that I was not really used to at the time. For example, affirmation from another woman - she gave me a lot of that. I saw someone who really believed in me; someone who knew I could be so much more than what I imagined. That is how a woman is supposed to be: they are meant to help you believe that you are so much more; to push your vision and build you. She was so encouraging, and she was much more passionate about God and the things of God than I was.

You could tell that she was a woman of integrity and spirituality, and that she was serious about her own Christian life and journey - at first, it was quite intimidating to be with her. Yet, at the same time, she was very humble. I realised that my intimidation was only because of the low self-esteem that I had built up from childhood. Here she was, so beautiful and confident - someone who knew what she wanted to do and where she wanted to go. She challenged me to envision bigger and better for my own life. I needed God's confidence to be with her, so I went back to the things that God had told me about being a victor, a son, etc. I had to remind myself of who I was. Identity affects relationships; it is another reason why we should know our purpose.

I thanked God that she was there to lead me to reflect on these things again. As our relationship grew, I found myself accepting certain aspects - that it was okay for me to be affirmed so much, to be encouraged - loved on so much. Apart from God and my mother, I had never experienced so much love and attention from anyone else. I accepted that I also deserved that attention. This time, it was good attention rather than the bad attention I had received before. This led me conclude that all these things contribute to one profound revelation: knowing who you are. If you don't know who you are, then you cannot even be with a woman. If you do not know who you are, then you cannot even handle a relationship, because a relationship only works if you know and can handle your own identity. If you do not have identity, there is no way you can have a healthy relationship with anyone.

So, knowing your purpose is crucial to everything you do in your life: Why do I exist? Why am I on this earth? Who am I to God? These are the questions that we should be asking. If I did not know this, I would not have been able to handle a relationship with my fiancée - that low self-esteem or lack of identity would have made me let her down. I would have told her there is no way we were going to work out. I would have just been intimidated by her and her success. I would have pulled away and not proposed. None of these things would have happened. This time, I was not facing people in ministry - I was facing this one person - my constant, always responsive to my emotions, to my thoughts and anything we were doing. I believe some inner healing was happening at this time. Both relational and female wounds were being touched.

The Purpose Of Existence

I truly believe that being with her was an experience that God wanted me to have, so that I could learn something new. It was His purpose - and that's how I knew that she was the one for me. That's how I knew that I wanted to work alongside her; that I wanted to have a future with her. She brought so many good qualities to my life: it was as though she raised me up from being a level 5 to a level 10 type of man. God used her at that time and now we look forward to the future. But there's only so much that God can do.

We must be mature enough to start applying those things that God has spoken into our lives, taking responsibility for them. In my own journey, I realised that I cannot run away from my problems; I have had to face them in order to move on. I have had to face every challenge and pass through the fire - through the valley, so that I can be where I'm supposed to be. God had done so many great things for me and this was yet another chapter where He taught me a great deal. I can say with all my heart that He has been good to me and all I can do is look forward to what He is going to do next. What is the next chapter for me? I have many dreams that can only be fulfilled through Him.

"We come to love not by finding a perfect person, but by learning to see an imperfect person perfectly."

CHAPTER 8
The New Me

I have gained so much confidence as I've struggled through my journey. Confidence is something that you build over time, and I certainly would not have developed this confidence without my experiences. They had to mould me and then God had to come and clean out the bad things in my life and re-shape me. I can now see God the Father has been doing this in me for years and years - and I can say that I have comfortably come to know for sure what I'm called to do and who I am in Christ. When God saves us, He also delivers us from the flawed self-image that we grow up with; He takes from us our false identity and replaces it with our true identity. This is exactly what He did for me, and I feel good about this, because no one can come and tell me otherwise.

I am confident in the positions that God has called me into: being a worshipper; a leader in the church... all those things are now things that I can say I fully own and have taken responsibility for. I no longer feel shaken in the areas I have talked about - I'm in a much stronger place, and God has brought me through a lot to get there. Brethren, this is where we all should be: we should be so confident in our purpose that no one can even shake the foundation. I know that I have crossed that bridge now, to a place where people can no longer define me; it is only God who can tell me who I am.

My circumstances do not change me. I have learnt the fundamentals of life. I have also found different passions and have been pursuing those things as well: other businesses, evangelism, salesmanship... you can see that the enemy wanted to shut me down when it came to people, but I'm called to these things. I can see now how my identity flaws would have spoilt my dreams of becoming a businessman, for instance, as business is all about people; it is relational.

So right now, I'm going after everything God has given me. I may not know the full picture of what it is God has called me to, but I know enough to follow the right path. Most importantly, I also know who I am in Him; I exercise those rights every day. When things come against me, I stand on the Word and the Truth. That is my continual stance, and it is paramount to my growth as a child of God.

Acts 17:28

"for in Him we live and move and exist, as even some of your own poets have said, 'For we also are His children."
[NASB]

This scripture tells us that our identity is in Him, and we can only progress or succeed if we partner with the identity He gave us. Without that knowledge, I cannot even move into the activities that I am engaged in right now. I just love how He has helped me; how He has brought me through. For those struggling to know who they are, I know that He really does have the answer for you. Even as I have pursued His purpose for my life, I have failed many times. I have questioned whether God really wants me to do any of it, whether I can do it at all, but because I *know* that it is what He has said, I am able to keep going, and because I *know* that I am his son, and that He is my Father, I *know* that I can succeed. That's what knowing your purpose is all about. Believe me, if you do not know your purpose, you cannot survive life. The enemy will toss you overboard again and again.

Many people go around doing what they want - what they like. That is because they do not know their purpose. The Bible says:

Proverbs 29: 18

"Where there is no vision, the people are unrestrained, but happy is he who keeps the law" [NASB].

The Bible tells us we need to have a vision. What is this vision it talks about? Your purpose is your vision; if you do not have a vision for your life, you will cast off all restraints: you will allow yourself to do anything. You will associate with anyone, you will not follow God, you will not follow your scroll, and you will thoughtlessly embrace whatever life brings to you. Hence, knowing your purpose helps you to live a life with restraint. That means that we live life carefully; we make meaningful decisions and we do only that which God has told us to do. And that's how it works - that's how it works now and that's what we need to know.

It is very important to know this, and I can only hope that each one of us can realise this - because God wants us to know who we are, but the enemy does not. The enemy knows that if we do not know our purpose, we will fall for every sin, every trap, and every temptation that he places in our way. He does not want us to know that we are sons of God, that we have power, that we have authority to rise above things, or that we can dive into the callings that God has given us. The enemy wants us to live a Christian life of mediocrity; God wants us to win.

"If you live for people's acceptance, you will die from their rejection."

— Lecrae

CHAPTER 9
Moving On

Moving on requires perceiving the next chapter of your life. I have come a long way; I have jumped through hoops and gone through valleys. This long journey of discovery has changed me into a person I would never have thought I could be. So, moving on is about going to the next level of maturity, seeing what else there is to pursue. I am still young, and I feel that God has allowed me to achieve many things, things that many people my age have not achieved. I am glad that God has made a table for me in the presence of my enemies and vindicated me before them, though differently to the way I thought it would be. The vengeance of God is the justice of God - He just doesn't do it the way we want it to be. Coming to know myself, knowing my purpose, and receiving His inner healing in my heart – this is the justice of God.

All this is God spreading a table for me in front of my enemies. He is showing me off; He is showing my oppressors that I can be more than I imagined for myself. That is how justice is served according to heaven. It is not about confrontations; it's not about hurting other people. God has brought me to such a good place. Right now, I feel like my eyes are open and I have a passion to help others who are lost in their identity. There are many kids I see on the street doing things that they are not supposed to do; I see many people in bad relationships, not taking God seriously and completely consumed by the things going on in their lives. My heart cries out for them, because I have a passion to help them see so much more, and I know God will give me a vision to help people in those situations, because I am called to help others find their true identities in Him.

Now I am just waiting on God to show me other avenues I can use to minister to those hearts. I can see that this is the greatest bondage in Christianity. I know many people say they are Christian, but there are only a few that can say that they know their purpose. Most are still lost, still blind even though they have been saved. A change needs to come - for the youth especially. A change needs to come to those who are in churches but feel lost. Most of all, change needs to come to the Church.

We need to start looking after one another - we should notice when one of us is troubled. We should know when to pull our friends out of pits and thus minister to them effectively. So, at the centre of my calling, there is a mission to show others that they too have an identity - that they too can make it; they too can fulfil their dreams. That is the calling of my life, woven into the very core of my being, and it will come out in everything I do. It will come out in business, it will come out in education, it will come out in my music; this message will be translated into every aspect of my life. It is God's will that we know who we are.

If you remember in the Garden of Eden, Adam lost his identity after the sin, and then God chastised him - not because he sinned, but because he lost his identity. He knew who he was before the sin, but after the sin, he had adopted so much shame and so much fear, that he lost who he was. He could not see that he was a son. God knew he couldn't entrust Adam with the things that he wanted to entrust him with; God gives an inheritance to those who know their true identity, because they are the ones who can be responsible.

We also fail because we lose sight of who we are, and we do not realise it. This is what brings defeat. Adam was bombarded with shame and fear and from that time, he could not recover. God could see that he had lost his position. He had left his position of sonship and moved into the position of an orphan. An orphan is someone who has no structure, does not know themselves and has no identity at all. When God called out, "Adam, where are you?" He knew exactly where Adam was. He was just showing him that he does not know himself anymore and that he had left his position of sonship.

You can see the significance of identity and purpose. I am always looking to know what the next level is for me. The good thing with God is that we keep growing - and we must keep growing. He continually showers us with His grace and power to help this happen. For me, moving on is moving into the next level of glory; the next level of maturity. That's where I want to get to and I know that as I get to those places of glory and maturity, I will understand more about my purpose, and do greater things for Christ.

"Every new beginning comes from some other beginning's end."

CHAPTER 10
A Word of Advice

My advice to you is that you do not skip these stages where God wants to show you who you are - and if you are not experiencing those seasons yet, I advise you to go and seek after them. I advise you to go and research the topic. Ask your leaders; ask them to show you how to find out about your purpose. This will really define your life, and you will find that you do not really have to live by what the enemy throws at you. You can overcome; you can jump over these things; move onto the next level; move onto the next bridge. It will shape everything about you. Trust me, you will never regret it. So, my advice to you is that this should be every Christians' goal: to discover your identity and purpose.

Even when you look at celebrities or anyone who is successful, the only reason they made it is because they understood and knew who they were and what they were meant to do. As a result, they have been able to reach their goal. Sadly, Christians have not learnt that lesson. The world knows it; everyone knows it; but not God's children. We go to church, Sunday after Sunday, but this can easily turn into a religious routine. God wants us to know Him deeper. He does not want us confined in the four walls of church. He wants us to be ministers in the world - those who evangelise in the world, doing what we were called to do, making Him known in the spheres of influence He has given us. Whether it is business, music or politics, we can bring His culture into those places. That is how it is meant to be.

So, I advise you to pursue these things in Heaven - all that we were called to be is written on what we call a Destiny Scroll. It is written in Heaven and I have found that many people are being able to go to Heaven and read their scroll. A scroll contains different aspects of your life. God shows what you are called to on that scroll. Whether it's education, business or music. The bible calls it, "the book of life." I can assure you that this is exactly what God would want you to do. If you look at the greatest heroes in the bible - Abraham, David, Joseph, Paul or Jesus; if you look at those distinct characters, you will see that they were peculiar and unique; they stood out because they knew who they were. And so they obeyed God with confidence. If you know who you are, you will also know who God is and you will naturally desire to follow Him and His ways. Jesus' faith never wavered because He knew who He was, He knew His purpose on earth and He knew what He was sent for. That should be our mission, brethren.

"Where there is no guidance the people fall,
But in abundance of counselors there is victory."

— Proverb 11:14

CHAPTER 11
Final Thoughts

I want to say my final thoughts, and I believe this is what God really wants to say to you now. God wants you to know that you, the reader, are more than you think. You have come from a distance; you have been tired, thirsty, lonely, and no one helped you on the way - even those who did try have left you. God wants you to know that He has been walking with you all along and even though you felt faint – even when you felt like you could not take the heat of the day and you felt as if what you were going through was unfair - He wants you to know that He was there beside you and He wants to deliver you. He wants to take you onto a different path. You have been walking in the desert for a long time. On this new path, He has placed better things for you there - you will find refreshment; you will find water; you will find food; friends; community - you will find so many different things that will nourish you. He wants to bring you from loneliness to fullness. He wants to lead you into many avenues in your life, but He is asking, "Will you follow me?" Will you follow all that He wants you to do? Will you seek after Him? For your identity only lies in Him. Your purpose lies in His hands. He knows it all - He knows how your future will end, He knows the beginning and the end. He knows those who are good for you; He knows those who are bad for you; He knows what path you should take and the one you should not take. So, He's asking you - will you trust Him in this season of your life?

No matter how hard it has been, will you trust Him? Will you follow His ways? He's calling you closer and closer to that place - so that you can be redeemed; so that He can know you; so that you can know Him better and better. With Him, there is water for you to drink that will fill you up like a fountain. This means that you can rely on Him for everything: for strength, for companionship, for vision, for direction (you don't have to direct yourself). He knows everything that is going on in your life. Even if you think you have bigger, better plans, His plans are always bigger than yours. He wants you to experience His plans; He wants you to experience the dreams He has for you.

God is asking us all, "Are you ready?" Are you ready to take the jump? Are you ready to discover who you are, will you come and spend time with me to find out? If you do, I will heal you, I will touch you, I will redeem you and that is the truth. I am who I am; I am the truth, the way and the life. I am the only one who will lead you to a better place. Everything you want to know; all your questions are in my hands. Every day I examine your heart and see the desires you hold there. I investigate them, and I say I am going to fulfil your desires and even though you do not see them manifest, they will manifest in my own time. Right now, I must get you ready - I have to take you from one place to another to change you, heal you, mould you and shape you. You are precious to me, so do not be afraid, because there's so much more for you to discover. Do not let your circumstances put you in a box. Do not let your circumstances trouble you. Just know that you have a Father who is closer than a friend; closer than a brother. That means you can do everything that you want. You can do all things through Him. In your hands I have given you a map, and that map will take you where you want to go. This means that I put all the answers in you. You can just ask me so that your spiritual eyes can open, so that you can see that map and so that you can see where you need

The Purpose Of Existence

to go. You cannot be dismayed, for everything you need is there. Knowing yourself is the greatest gift ever; knowing yourself is also loving yourself, and when you love yourself you will be able to love Me - and when you love Me, you will experience a new level of freedom. You will find that you will be so liberated: free from religion, free from fear, free from corruption, free from distractions. You will be so free; My love will guide you always.

ABOUT THE AUTHOR

Claver Lukoki is a deacon and a worshipper at the Act of Faith Ministries. Following his experience with the Lord, learning to love himself and understanding his purpose, he is now a motivational speaker. He has a passion for the body of Christ and is driven to impact and empower individuals to live a purpose-filled life.

He is also a gospel artist, through his love for music and the anointing placed upon his life, he hosts several conferences and music shows. Claver journeys through various conferences ministering through songs with a sensitive heart, aiming to help those who have a desire to know why they are here on earth, to know why they were created.

Claver addresses critical issues affecting the full range of human, social, and spiritual development. The central theme of his message is the understanding of the purpose of human's that are confined to the vision of their lives.

He is the founder and president of B.M.A foundation which aims to also build and empower young people. He is the holder of a bachelor's degree in Media from the University of Bedfordshire.

To Contact Claver Lukoki:
Email: purposeofexistence@hotmail.com
Facebook: Claver Lukoki
Instagram: Claver Lukoki

Greater Works International Publishing Company

A Unique publishing company that aims to help authors through the process of writing. We have a group of experts involved in editing, ghost writing, and proofreading. We help authors find out God's heart for their book and with their permission, our team are able to give prophetic input and suggestions to the concept of the book. Our heart is that everyone writes the book that God ordained them to write and that they do this in the right season and time. We work closely with the author to make sure that their signature and heart are visible through the book.

Get in touch with us;

www.greaterworkspublishing.com

Email:
admin@greaterworkspublishing.com

www.ingramcontent.com/pod-product-compliance
Lightning Source LLC
Chambersburg PA
CBHW052111070526
44584CB00017B/2430